AROUND TOWN

FARMER'S MARKET

by Adeline J. Zimmerman

TABLE OF CONTENTS

tadpole books

WORDS TO KNOW

buy

farmer

flowers

fruit

market

vegetables

FARMER'S MARKET

Let's go to the market!

We see fruit.

5

We see vegetables.

We see flowers.

We see a farmer!

She grows this food.

She lets us try some.

We buy food for dinner.

Yum!

LET'S REVIEW!

What is this family buying at the farmer's market?

INDEX